ANIMALS OF THE ARCTIC

Narwhals

by Betsy Rathburn

BELLWETHER MEDIA • MINNEAPOLIS, MN

Blastoff! Readers are carefully developed by literacy experts to build reading stamina and move students toward fluency by combining standards-based content with developmentally appropriate text.

Level 1 provides the most support through repetition of high-frequency words, light text, predictable sentence patterns, and strong visual support.

Level 2 offers early readers a bit more challenge through varied sentences, increased text load, and text-supportive special features.

Level 3 advances early-fluent readers toward fluency through increased text load, less reliance on photos, advancing concepts, longer sentences, and more complex special features.

★ **Blastoff! Universe**

Reading Level

Grade **K**

Grades **1–3**

Grade **4**

This edition first published in 2021 by Bellwether Media, Inc.

No part of this publication may be reproduced in whole or in part without written permission of the publisher. For information regarding permission, write to Bellwether Media, Inc., Attention: Permissions Department, 6012 Blue Circle Drive, Minnetonka, MN 55343.

Library of Congress Cataloging-in-Publication Data

Names: Rathburn, Betsy, author.
Title: Narwhals / Betsy Rathburn.
Description: Minneapolis, MN : Bellwether Media, Inc., 2021. | Series: Blast off! readers: animals of the Arctic | Includes bibliographical references and index. | Audience: Ages 5-8 | Audience: Grades K-1 | Summary: "Relevant images match informative text in this introduction to narwhals. Intended for students in kindergarten through third grade"-- Provided by publisher.
Identifiers: LCCN 2019054179 (print) | LCCN 2019054180 (ebook) | ISBN 9781644872130 (library binding) | ISBN 9781618919717 (ebook)
Subjects: LCSH: Narwhal--Juvenile literature. | Zoology--Arctic regions--Juvenile literature.
Classification: LCC QL737.C433 R38 2021 (print) | LCC QL737.C433 (ebook) | DDC 599.5/43--dc23
LC record available at https://lccn.loc.gov/2019054179
LC ebook record available at https://lccn.loc.gov/2019054180

Text copyright © 2021 by Bellwether Media, Inc. BLASTOFF! READERS and associated logos are trademarks and/or registered trademarks of Bellwether Media, Inc.

Editor: Kieran Downs   Designer: Brittany McIntosh

Printed in the United States of America, North Mankato, MN

Table of Contents

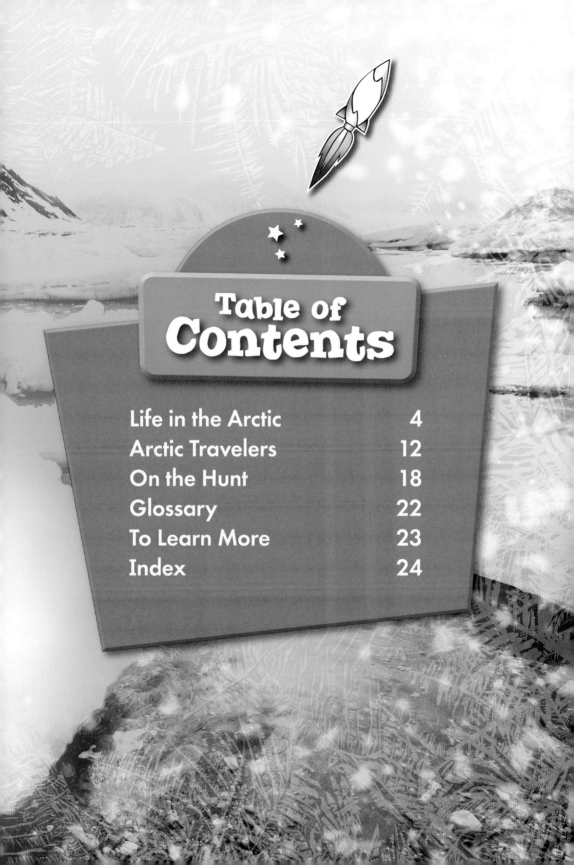

Life in the Arctic

tusk

Narwhals are the unicorns of the sea! They are known for their long **tusks**.

These **mammals** swim through the Arctic Ocean.

Narwhal Range

range =

N
W — E
S

The Arctic **biome** is very cold. But these whales stay warm.

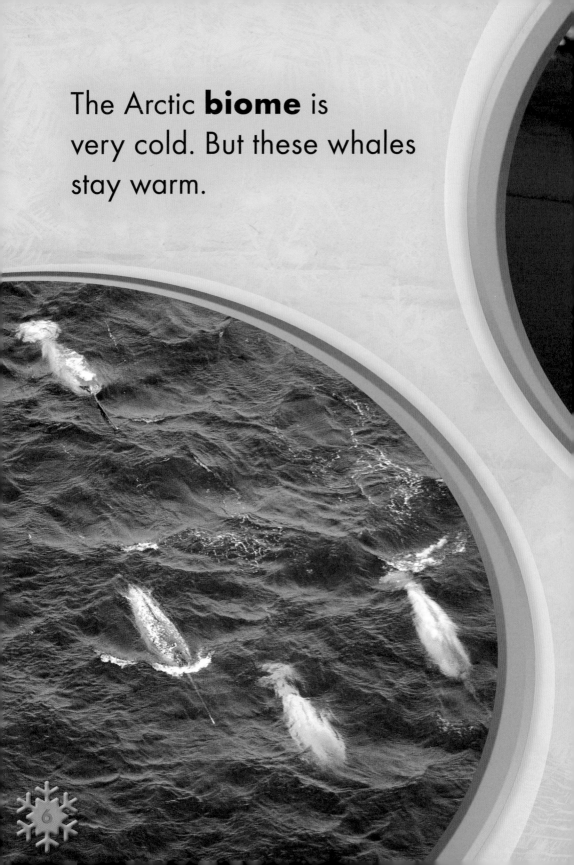

Thick **blubber** covers their bodies. It keeps in heat!

Male narwhals have tusks. Some females do, too.

Tusks help the whales find **mates**. They may also help catch **prey**!

Special Adaptations

blowhole

long tusk

thick blubber

The Arctic is full of **predators**.
Narwhals must be careful.

Their necks can turn easily.
This helps the whales
spot enemies!

Arctic Travelers

Narwhals look for holes in the Arctic ice. They come up to breathe through their **blowholes**.

blowhole

12

They also make breathing holes
by breaking ice with their heads.

Narwhals **migrate** in the winter. They look for places with thin ice.

They use **echolocation**
to find their way!

Narwhals swim in **pods**.
Pods may join into large
herds to migrate.

Herds may hold hundreds
of these whales! They
click and squeak to talk
to each other.

pod

Narwhal Stats

Least Concern	Near Threatened	Vulnerable	Endangered	Critically Endangered	Extinct in the Wild	Extinct

conservation status: least concern

life span: up to 55 years

herd

17

On the Hunt

Narwhals are good hunters.
They use sound to find food.

They like to eat fish
and shrimp.

Narwhal Diet

Arctic cod

northern
prawn

Gonatus squids

Narwhals do not have many teeth. They suck in water to catch prey.

Sometimes they **stun** food with their tusks. These Arctic whales find plenty to eat!

Glossary

biome—a large area with certain plants, animals, and weather

blowholes—holes on the heads of dolphins or whales that let air in and out

blubber—the layer of body fat that helps cold water animals stay warm

echolocation—the act of sending out sounds and listening for the echoes to find distant objects

herds—groups of animals that live and travel together

mammals—warm-blooded animals that have backbones and feed their young milk

mates—partners

migrate—to move from one place to another, often with the seasons

pods—groups of narwhals

predators—animals that hunt other animals for food

prey—animals that are hunted by other animals for food

stun—to make senseless or dizzy by a blow

tusks—long teeth that come out of the mouth

To Learn More

AT THE LIBRARY

Hansen, Grace. *Narwhal*. Minneapolis, Minn.: Abdo Kids, 2020.

Nugent, Samantha. *Arctic Ocean*. New York, N.Y.: AV2 by Weigl, 2018.

Rathburn, Betsy. *Beluga Whales*. Minneapolis, Minn.: Bellwether Media, 2021.

ON THE WEB

FACTSURFER

Factsurfer.com gives you a safe, fun way to find more information.

1. Go to www.factsurfer.com.

2. Enter "narwhals" into the search box and click 🔍.

3. Select your book cover to see a list of related content.

Index